Symphony No. 6
in B Minor, Op. 74
("Pathétique")

Symphony No. 6
in B Minor, Op. 74
("Pathétique")

Peter Ilyitch
TCHAIKOVSKY

DOVER PUBLICATIONS, INC.
Mineola, New York

Published in Canada by General Publishing Company, Ltd., 30 Lesmill Road, Don Mills, Toronto, Ontario.

Published in the United Kingdom by Constable and Company, Ltd., 3 The Lanchesters, 162–164 Fulham Palace Road, London W6 9ER.

Bibliographical Note

This Dover edition, first published in 1997, is a republication of the work originally published by Breitkopf & Härtel, Leipzig, n.d.

International Standard Book Number: 0-486-29954-6

Manufactured in the United States of America
Dover Publications, Inc., 31 East 2nd Street, Mineola, N.Y. 11501

CONTENTS

To Vladimir Davidov

Symphony No. 6
in B Minor, Op. 74
("Pathétique")
(1893)

INSTRUMENTATION

3 Flutes [Flöten, Fl.]
Flute 3 doubles Piccolo [Kleine Flöte, Kl. Fl.]
2 Oboes [Oboen, Ob.]
2 Clarinets in A [Klarinetten, Klar.]
2 Bassoons [Fagotte, Fag.]

4 Horns in F [Hörner, Hrn.]
2 Trumpets in A, B♭ ("B") [Trompeten, Trp.]
3 Trombones [Posaunen, Pos.
(Alt, Tenor, Baß / A., T., B.]

Timpani [Pauken, Pk.]

Percussion
   Bass Drum and Cymbals
      [Grosse Trommel, Gr. Tr. u(nd) Becken]
   Tam-tam *(ad libitum)* [Tamt(am)]

Violins 1, 2 [Violine, Viol.]
Violas [Viola, Vla.]
Cellos [Violoncell, Vc.]
Basses [Kontrabaß, Kb.]

Symphony No. 6
in B Minor, Op. 74
("Pathétique")

I

2

6

12

16

243
N
1.
Fl.
2.
Kl.Fl.
Ob. 1. 2
1. in A
Klar.
2. in A
Fag. 1. 2
1. 2. in F
Hrn.
3. 4. in F
Trp. 1. 2
in B
A. T.
Pos.
B.
Btb.
Pk.
N
Viol. 1
Viol. 2
Vla.
Vc.
Kb.
N

39

II

52

58

66

111
1.
Fl.
2.
3.
Ob.1.2
Klar.
Fag.1.2
Hrn.
B Pos.
Viol.1
Viol.2
Vla.
Vc.
Kb.
div.
a2
mf
più f
div.
unis.
pizz.
arco
117
K
f
mp
p
pizz.

III

Allegro molto vivace (♩. = 152)
1. Flöten 2.
Kleine Flöte
Oboen 1.2
1. in A Klarinetten 2. in A
Fagotte 1.2
1.2. in F Hörner 3.4. in F
Trompeten 1.2 in A
Alt, Tenor Posaunen Baß
Baßtuba
Pauken in Fis, G, H
Gr. Trommel u. Becken
Allegro molto vivace (♩. = 152)
Violine 1 divisi
Violine 2 divisi
Viola divisi
Violoncell divisi
Kontrabaß divisi
Allegro molto vivace (♩. = 152)

5
A
1.
Fl.
2.
Ob.1.2
1.in A
Klar.
2.in A
Fag.1.2
Hrn.
1.2.in F
Viol.1
div.
Viol.2
div.
Vla.
div.
Vc.
div.
Kb.
div.

36
1.
Fl.
2.
Kl. Fl.
1. in A
Klar.
2. in A
Fag. 1.2
Viol. 1
div.
Viol. 2
div.
Vla.
div.
Vc.
div.
Kb.
div.
pizz.
arco
p
mf

41
E
1.
Fl.
2.
Kl. Fl.
1. in A
Klar.
2. in A
Fag. 1.2
Hrn.
1.2. in F
Trp. 1.2
in A
A.-T. Pos.
Pk.
Viol. 1
div.
Viol. 2
div.
Vla.
div.
Vc.
div.
Kb.
div.
marcato
arco
pizz.
mp
mf
p
f

56
1.
Fl.
2.
Kl.Fl.
a 2
Ob.1.2
1. in A
Klar.
2. in A
Fag.1.2
crescendo
1.2. in F
Hrn.
3.4. in F
Trp.1.2
in A
A.
Pos.
B.
Pk.
Viol.1
Viol.2
Vla.
Vc.
Kb.

61
G
1.
Fl.
2.
Kl. Fl.
Ob. 1.2
a 2
1. in A
Klar.
2. in A
Fag. 1.2
1.2. in F
Hrn.
3. in F
Trp. 1.2 in A
A. T.
Pos.
B.
Btb.
Pk.
Viol. 1
Viol. 2
Vla.
Vc.
Kb.
poco a poco crescendo
p crescendo
p crescendo
mf crescendo
crescendo poco a poco
p
mp
mf

66
Fl. 1.
2.
Kl.Fl.
Ob.1.2
Klar. 1.in A
2.in A
Fag.1.2
Hrn. 1.2.in F
3.4.in F
Trp. 1.2.in A
Pos. A.T.
B.
Btb.
Pk.
Gr.Tr.
Viol.1
Viol.2
Vla.
Vc.
Kb.
a 2
f cresc.
diminuendo
muta in G,A,D
dim.

140
1.
Fl.
2.
Ob.1.2
1.in A
Klar.
2.in A
Fag.1.2
Hrn.1.2
in F
Viol.1
div.
Viol.2
div.
Vla.
div.
Vc.
div.
Kb.
pizz.
arco
div.

145
1.
Fl.
2.
Ob.1.2
1.in A
Klar.
2.in A
Fag.1.2
Hrn.1.2 in F
Viol.1 div.
Viol.2 div.
Vla. div.
Vc. div.
Kb.
poco cresc.
pizz.
arco
p
mp

171
1. in A
Klar.
2. in A
Fag. 1.2
2. in F
Hrn.
4. in F
Viol. 1 div.
Viol. 2 div.
Vla. div.
Vc. div.
Kb. div.
pizz.
arco
diminuendo

175
1.
Fl.
2.
Kl. Fl.
1. in A
Klar.
2. in A
Fag. 1.2
A.-T.-Pos.
Pk.
Viol. 1
div.
Viol. 2
div.
Vla.
div.
Vc.
div.
Kb.
div.
arco
pizz.

189
T
1.
Fl.
2.
Kl. Fl.
Ob. 1. 2
a 2
1. in A
Klar.
2. in A
Fag. 1. 2
Hrn.
Trp. 1. 2
in A
A. T.
Pos.
B.
Btb.
Pk.
Viol. 1
div.
Viol. 2
div.
Vla.
div.
Vc.
div.
Kb.
div.

194
1.
Fl.
2.
Ob. 1. 2
1. in A
Klar.
2. in A
Fag. 1. 2
1. 2 in F
Hrn.
3. 4 in F
Trp. 1. 2 in A
A. T.
Pos.
B.
Btb.
Pk.
Viol. 1
Viol. 2
Vla.
Vc.
Kb.
leggieramente
pp
a 2
unis.

201
U
1.
Fl.
2.
p leggieramente
leggieramente
a 2
Klar.
Hrn.
p poco a poco cresc.
A. T.
Pos.
B.
Btb.
Pk.
poco a poco
Viol. 1
Viol. 2
div.
Vla.
Vc.
Kb.

211
1.
Fl.
2.
Kl. Fl.
Ob. 1. 2
1. in A
Klar.
2. in A
Fag. 1. 2
1. 2. in F
Hrn.
3. 4. in F
Trp. 1. 2
in A
A. T.
Pos.
B.
Btb.
Pk.
Viol. 1
Viol. 2
Vla.
Vc.
Kb.

216
W
1.
Fl.
2.
Kl. Fl.
Ob. 1.2
1. in A
Klar.
2. in A
a 2
Fag. 1.2
1. 2. in F
Hrn.
3. 4. in F
Trp. 1.2
in A
A. T.
Pos.
B.
Btb.
Pk.
Viol. 1
Viol. 2
Vla.
Vc.
Kb.

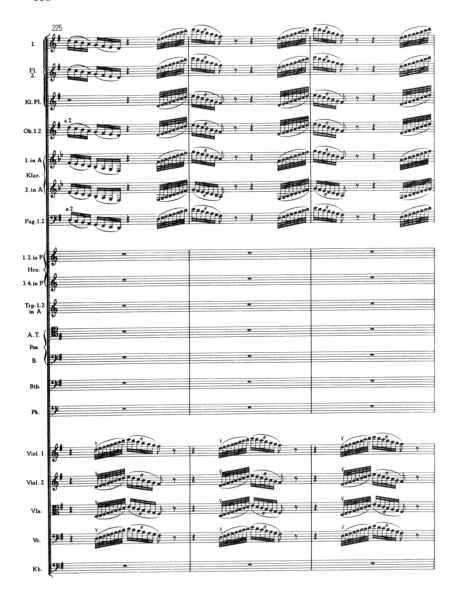

228
Y
1.
Fl.
2.
Kl. Fl.
Ob. 1. 2
a 2
1. in A
Klar.
2. in A
Fag. 1. 2
1. 2. in F
Hrn.
3. 4. in F
Trp. 1. 2
in A
A. T.
Pos.
B.
Btb.
Pk.
Viol. 1
Viol. 2
Vla.
Vc.
Kb.
fff

118

(Die Becken dürfen nicht angebunden sein)

121

122

274
DD
1.
Fl.
2.
Kl. Fl.
Ob. 1. 2
1. in A
Klar.
2. in A
Fag. 1. 2
1. 2. in F
Hrn.
3. 4. in F
Trp. 1. 2
in A
A. T.
Pos.
B.
Btb.
Pk.
Gr. Tr.
a 2
marcato assai
marcato assai
DD
Viol. 1
Viol. 2
Vla.
Vc.
Kb.
DD

130

137

138

341
1.
Fl.
2.
Kl. Fl.
Ob. 1.2
1. in A
Klar.
2. in A
Fag. 1.2
a 2
1. 2. in F
Hrn.
3. 4. in F
Trp. 1.2
in A
A. T.
Pos.
B.
Btb.
Pk.
Gr. Tr.
fff
Viol. 1
Viol. 2
Vla.
Vc.
Kb.

IV. Finale

146

149

154

155

156

END OF EDITION

DOVER FULL-SIZE
ORCHESTRAL SCORES

THE SIX BRANDENBURG CONCERTOS AND THE FOUR ORCHESTRAL SUITES IN FULL SCORE, Johann Sebastian Bach. Complete standard Bach-Gesellschaft editions in large, clear format. Study score. 273pp. 9 × 12. 23376-6 Pa. **$11.95**

COMPLETE CONCERTI FOR SOLO KEYBOARD AND ORCHESTRA IN FULL SCORE, Johann Sebastian Bach. Bach's seven complete concerti for solo keyboard and orchestra in full score from the authoritative Bach-Gesellschaft edition. 206pp. 9 × 12.
24929-8 Pa. **$11.95**

THE THREE VIOLIN CONCERTI IN FULL SCORE, Johann Sebastian Bach. Concerto in A Minor, BWV 1041; Concerto in E Major, BWV 1042; and Concerto for Two Violins in D Minor, BWV 1043. Bach-Gesellschaft edition. 64pp. 9⅜ × 12¼. 25124-1 Pa. **$6.95**

GREAT ORGAN CONCERTI, OPP. 4 & 7, IN FULL SCORE, George Frideric Handel. 12 organ concerti composed by great Baroque master are reproduced in full score from the *Deutsche Handelgesellschaft* edition. 138pp. 9⅜ × 12¼. 24462-8 Pa. **$8.95**

COMPLETE CONCERTI GROSSI IN FULL SCORE, George Frideric Handel. Monumental Opus 6 Concerti Grossi, Opus 3 and "Alexander's Feast" Concerti Grossi—19 in all—reproduced from most authoritative edition. 258pp. 9⅜ × 12¼. 24187-4 Pa. **$13.95**

LATER SYMPHONIES, Wolfgang A. Mozart. Full orchestral scores to last symphonies (Nos. 35–41) reproduced from definitive Breitkopf & Härtel Complete Works edition. Study score. 285pp. 9 × 12.
23052-X Pa. **$12.95**

PIANO CONCERTOS NOS. 17–22, Wolfgang Amadeus Mozart. Six complete piano concertos in full score, with Mozart's own cadenzas for Nos. 17–19. Breitkopf & Härtel edition. Study score. 370pp. 9⅜ × 12¼.
23599-8 Pa. **$16.95**

PIANO CONCERTOS NOS. 23–27, Wolfgang Amadeus Mozart. Mozart's last five piano concertos in full score, plus cadenzas for Nos. 23 and 27, and the Concert Rondo in D Major, K.382. Breitkopf & Härtel edition. Study score. 310pp. 9⅜ × 12¼. 23600-5 Pa. **$13.95**

CONCERTI FOR WIND INSTRUMENTS IN FULL SCORE, Wolfgang Amadeus Mozart. Exceptional volume contains ten pieces for orchestra and wind instruments and includes some of Mozart's finest, most popular music. 272pp. 9⅜ × 12¼. 25228-0 Pa. **$13.95**

SYMPHONIES 88–92 IN FULL SCORE: The Haydn Society Edition, Joseph Haydn. Full score of symphonies Nos. 88 through 92. Large, readable noteheads, ample margins for fingerings, etc., and extensive Editor's Commentary. 304pp. 9 × 12. (Available in U.S. only)
24445-8 Pa. **$15.95**

THE RITE OF SPRING IN FULL SCORE, Igor Stravinsky. A reprint of the original full-score edition of the most famous musical work of the 20th century, created as a ballet score for Diaghilev's Ballets Russes. 176pp. 9⅜ × 12¼. (Available in U.S. only) 25857-2 Pa. **$9.95**

FOUR SYMPHONIES IN FULL SCORE, Franz Schubert. Schubert's four most popular symphonies: No. 4 in C Minor ("Tragic"); No. 5 in B-flat Major; No. 8 in B Minor ("Unfinished"); and No. 9 in C Major ("Great"). Breitkopf & Härtel edition. Study score. 261pp. 9⅜ × 12¼.
23681-1 Pa. **$13.95**

GREAT OVERTURES IN FULL SCORE, Carl Maria von Weber. Overtures to *Oberon, Der Freischutz, Euryanthe* and *Preciosa* reprinted from auhoritative Breitkopf & Härtel editions. 112pp. 9 × 12.
25225-6 Pa. **$9.95**

SYMPHONIES NOS. 1, 2, 3, AND 4 IN FULL SCORE, Ludwig van Beethoven. Republication of H. Litolff edition. 272pp. 9 × 12.
26033-X Pa. **$11.95**

SYMPHONIES NOS. 5, 6 AND 7 IN FULL SCORE, Ludwig van Beethoven. Republication of the H. Litolff edition. 272pp. 9 × 12.
26034-8 Pa. **$11.95**

SYMPHONIES NOS. 8 AND 9 IN FULL SCORE, Ludwig van Beethoven. Republication of the H. Litolff edition. 256pp. 9 × 12.
26035-6 Pa. **$11.95**

SIX GREAT OVERTURES IN FULL SCORE, Ludwig van Beethoven. Six staples of the orchestral repertoire from authoritative Breitkopf & Härtel edition. *Leonore Overtures,* Nos. 1–3; Overtures to *Coriolanus, Egmont, Fidelio.* 288pp. 9 × 12. 24789-9 Pa. **$13.95**

COMPLETE PIANO CONCERTOS IN FULL SCORE, Ludwig van Beethoven. Complete scores of five great Beethoven piano concertos, with all cadenzas as he wrote them, reproduced from authoritative Breitkopf & Härtel edition. New table of contents. 384pp. 9⅜ × 12¼.
24563-2 Pa. **$15.95**

THREE ORCHESTRAL WORKS IN FULL SCORE: Academic Festival Overture, Tragic Overture and Variations on a Theme by Joseph Haydn, Johannes Brahms. Reproduced from the authoritative Breitkopf & Härtel edition three of Brahms's great orchestral favorites. Editor's commentary in German and English. 112pp. 9⅜ × 12¼.
24637-X Pa. **$8.95**

COMPLETE CONCERTI IN FULL SCORE, Johannes Brahms. Piano Concertos Nos. 1 and 2; Violin Concerto, Op. 77; Concerto for Violin and Cello, Op. 102. Definitive Breitkopf & Härtel edition. 352pp. 9⅜ × 12¼.
24170-X Pa. **$15.95**

COMPLETE SYMPHONIES IN FULL SCORE, Robert Schumann. No. 1 in B-flat Major, Op. 38 ("Spring"); No. 2 in C Major, Op. 61; No. 3 in E Flat Major, Op. 97 ("Rhenish"); and No. 4 in D Minor, Op. 120. Breitkopf & Härtel editions. Study score. 416pp. 9⅜ × 12¼.
24013-4 Pa. **$18.95**

GREAT WORKS FOR PIANO AND ORCHESTRA IN FULL SCORE, Robert Schumann. Collection of three superb pieces for piano and orchestra, including the popular Piano Concerto in A Minor. Breitkopf & Härtel edition. 183pp. 9⅜ × 12¼.
24340-0 Pa. **$10.95**

THE PIANO CONCERTOS IN FULL SCORE, Frédéric Chopin. The authoritative Breitkopf & Härtel full-score edition in one volume of Piano Concertos No. 1 in E Minor and No. 2 in F Minor. 176pp. 9 × 12.
25835-1 Pa. **$10.95**

THE PIANO CONCERTI IN FULL SCORE, Franz Liszt. Available in one volume the Piano Concerto No. 1 in E-flat Major and the Piano Concerto No. 2 in A Major—are among the most studied, recorded and performed of all works for piano and orchestra. 144pp. 9 × 12.
25221-3 Pa. **$8.95**

SYMPHONY NO. 8 IN G MAJOR, OP. 88, SYMPHONY NO. 9 IN E MINOR, OP. 95 ("NEW WORLD") IN FULL SCORE, Antonín Dvořák. Two celebrated symphonies by the great Czech composer, the Eighth and the immensely popular Ninth, "From the New World" in one volume. 272pp. 9 × 12.
24749-X Pa. **$13.95**

FOUR ORCHESTRAL WORKS IN FULL SCORE: Rapsodie Espagnole, Mother Goose Suite, Valses Nobles et Sentimentales, and Pavane for a Dead Princess, Maurice Ravel. Four of Ravel's most popular orchestral works, reprinted from original full-score French editions. 240pp. 9⅜ × 12¼. (Not available in France or Germany)
25962-5 Pa. **$12.95**

DAPHNIS AND CHLOE IN FULL SCORE, Maurice Ravel. Definitive full-score edition of Ravel's rich musical setting of a Greek fable by Longus is reprinted here from the original French edition. 320pp. 9⅜ × 12¼. (Not available in France or Germany) 25826-2 Pa. **$15.95**

THREE GREAT ORCHESTRAL WORKS IN FULL SCORE, Claude Debussy. Three favorites by influential modernist: *Prélude à l'Après-midi d'un Faune, Nocturnes,* and *La Mer.* Reprinted from early French editions. 279pp. 9 × 12. 24441-5 Pa. **$13.95**

SYMPHONY IN D MINOR IN FULL SCORE, César Franck. Superb, authoritative edition of Franck's only symphony, an often-performed and recorded masterwork of late French romantic style. 160pp. 9 × 12. 25373-2 Pa. **$9.95**

THE GREAT WALTZES IN FULL SCORE, Johann Strauss, Jr. Complete scores of eight melodic masterpieces: The Beautiful Blue Danube, Emperor Waltz, Tales of the Vienna Woods, Wiener Blut, four more. Authoritative editions. 336pp. 8⅜ × 11¼. 26009-7 Pa. **$14.95**

THE FIREBIRD IN FULL SCORE (Original 1910 Version), Igor Stravinsky. Handsome, inexpensive edition of modern masterpiece, renowned for brilliant orchestration, glowing color. Authoritative Russian edition. 176pp. 9⅜ × 12¼. (Available in U.S. only) 25535-2 Pa. **$10.95**

PETRUSHKA IN FULL SCORE: Original Version, Igor Stravinsky. The definitive full-score edition of Stravinsky's masterful score for the great Ballets Russes 1911 production of *Petrushka.* 160pp. 9⅜ × 12¼. (Available in U.S. only) 25680-4 Pa. **$9.95**